WORDS ALONG THE WAY

Wisdom, Hope, & Encouragement for Your Journey

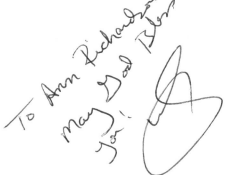

UMIKO D. JONES SR.

Limits of Liability and Disclaimer of Warranty

Cover Design: Studio 5 Agency (www.studio5agency.com)

Printed in the United States of America

ISBN 978-1-948270-25-0

Keen Vision Publishing, LLC
www.keen-vision.com

This book is dedicated to...

The memory of my beloved grandmother, Mrs. Genola Moore, whose love, wisdom and example helped to shape my life and ministry.

The memory of my mother, the late Ms. Gloria Jean Jones, whose struggle to overcome the many obstacles in her life taught me to be both resilient and determined.

My children, Umiko II, Timothy & Talia – It is my greatest honor to be your father. I pray that I will make each of you as proud as you make me.

Every "Kingdom Connection", that I have been privileged to make, from my years of formation at the Zion Hill Church in Milwaukee, WI to the saints the Lord has assigned to my hands at the Gravel Hill Church, thank you for every word of wisdom, correction, kindness and encouragement.

My family and friends both near and far, thank you...for everything.

You, the reader, may you be strengthened & encouraged along your way.

CONTENTS

INTRODUCTION

Life has a way of getting the best of us. Regardless of the amount of intestinal fortitude we possess or how greatly determined we may be – life happens. Discouragement, frustration, and irritation attack us as we journey through every season of life.

In Luke 24, two disciples are journeying together toward Emmaus discussing the events of the previous days. It has been three days since Jesus was crucified, and they have been gripped by sadness. As they walk, Jesus comes along and begins talking with them. Even though they did not recognize Him, His words provide clarity and strength for them.

From time to time, we all need words of encouragement or clarity to strengthen us on our journey. *Words Along the Way* provides you an opportunity to receive strength, wisdom, and renewed hope. Each devotional contains a brief scriptural lesson and a prayer focus. Read them in order or skip around to get the word you need to help you along the way.

SOMETHING WORTH
SHOUTING ABOUT

O clap your hands, all ye people;
shout unto God with the voice of triumph.
Psalm 47:1(KJV)

P eople shout, yell, and scream about many things. At a football or basketball game, there is much shouting. Visit the Congress or Senate as they debate a challenging bill and you'll find plenty of yelling. In homes all across the world, husbands and wives are shouting, and kids are screaming. For most, the more important an issue is, the louder they become. When the excitement of a moment builds, speaking loudly becomes an inevitable for many. Truth be told, many of the things we shout about really aren't that important.

In Psalms 47, the psalmist opens by exhorting us to clap our hands and shout to God with triumphant voices. This Psalm expresses jubilation at the majesty of God and His power to subdue nations. Likely written as an outflow of Jehoshaphat's victory over Moab, Ammon, and Mount Seir in II Chronicles 20, the writer celebrates the enthronement of a Sovereign God who rules over all the earth. He indicates to us that when we consider our God and all His deeds, it should evoke a level of worship and praise that would make a ballgame sound like a library.

Our God is great and He is greatly to be praised! His greatness is seen throughout human history. From the beginning, He is God. Eternal. Immutable. Omnipotent. He has always been and will always be God. There is nothing beyond His control. He is infinitely God. Though He is unlimited in power and resources, He created everything we see with just the sound of His voice. Despite His sovereignty, He still shows great concern about even the smallest details of our lives. Now THAT is something worth shouting about!

Father, we pause today to celebrate your greatness. You are mighty and magnificent. There is no one like you. We thank You for being our God, deliverer, protector, and defender. You supply our needs, look beyond our faults, and give us endless mercies daily. We love you.

HOPE **IN GOD**

Why art thou cast down, O my soul?
and why art thou disquieted in me?
Hope thou in God: for I shall yet praise him
for the help of His countenance.
Psalm 42:5 (KJV)

Hope is a small word armed with significant power and impact. Hope fuels dreams and aspirations. Hope gives focus to those who sit in the waiting rooms of hospitals and doctor's offices awaiting the outcome of surgeries, procedures, tests, and diagnoses. Hope empowers the timid, energizes the faithful, and provides support during some of the most difficult seasons of our lives.

In our scripture focus, the psalmist is experiencing a difficult season in his life. In the preceding verses, he expresses his longing for God and his desire to worship Him in the Temple. Exiled and surrounded by captors who mock him and question his God's existence, the psalmist is experiencing a season of discouragement. In the midst of this, he determines that he will have hope in God and he will praise God in spite of his current condition.

We all experience moments of discouragement. Along our journey, we will be surrounded by those who doubt our God and mock our faith. Regardless of this, our hope is in God. Think about all that God has already done in your life. No, really stop and take a moment to think about it. All that you have, all that you are, and all that you will ever be is because of God. In all the accidents you've avoided, dangers you've come through, and near death experiences that made your life pass before your very eyes, you were preserved because of God's grace, mercy, and will! Knowing this, we can look forward with great confidence to what God will do!

Father, thank you for reminding us that we can hope in you. Thank you for walking with us through every season of our lives. Even when we are experiencing discouragement, we know you will see us through. Shield our ears from the voices of those who speak doubt and unbelief. This day, we choose to focus our attention on you and give you the praise.

YOU CAN DO IT

Then he answered and spake unto me, saying,
This is the word of the LORD unto Zerubbabel,
saying, Not by might, nor by power, but by my
spirit, Saith the LORD of hosts.
Zechariah 4:6 (KJV)

God never asks us to do things we are fully capable of accomplishing in our own strength. Most of the time, when we are given assignments, we find ourselves trying to figure out how we should get it done. *Where do I get the resources? What if I can't find support? When is the right time to begin?* Our list of questions can be endless.

In our passage, Zerubbabel is tasked with rebuilding the Temple. It was an enormous undertaking. There was a great deal of work to be done. God sends His word to encourage Zerubbabel that the work will be accomplished. God tells him that it won't be done by military strength (might), nor will it be accomplished by human manpower (power). The key to his success will be supplied by the Spirit of God.

7

Has God given you any tasks that you find overwhelming? Perhaps you have been wondering how you are going to get it done. In the back of your mind you may be wondering, *"How could God ask ME to do this? Doesn't He know that I'm not capable of handling this?"* Maybe you have been working toward that vision, but things don't seem to be connecting like you thought they would. God's Word is clear: Our success comes from the Spirit of God. Regardless of the strength or support we have or lack, when we rely on God, we cannot fail.

Lord, help us as we seek to complete the assignments you have given us. Sometimes, we feel overwhelmed, but today, we rededicate ourselves to you and recommit to the assignment. We know that we will be successful as we rely on your spirit to supply us with what we need.

A NEW THING

See, I am doing a new thing! Now it springs up;
do you not perceive it? I am making a way
in the wilderness and streams in the wasteland.
Isaiah 43:19 (NIV)

E veryone likes new things. Nothing compares to the excitement of having something new. The smell of a new car, buying a new house, purchasing new clothes, wearing new jewelry, or even trying a new restaurant gives us an unexplainable rush. The anticipation of starting a new job, the butterflies we feel when starting a new relationship, the awe and wonder of a new baby, and even venturing through a new city is exciting. Newness breaks up the monotony of the mundane.

Israel has been in captivity for some time now. While their captivity is a direct result of their disobedience, the children of Israel are still in need of some encouragement. Isaiah spent much time delineating the rising and falling of Israel through many periods of captivity in the first half of this book. However, beginning in Isaiah 40, he began to speak about God's deliverance and redemption. In the midst of much uncertainty about God's intentions toward His people, Isaiah reminds us in Isaiah 43:19, not to become so focused on the past that we miss what God is doing now.

Look around you today and see what the Lord is doing in YOUR life. Don't become so engrossed in the negative that you miss the new thing God is doing. Though it may be difficult to perceive, know that God is up to something in your life. Seek Him, inquire of Him, and trust Him. God indeed makes ways in the wilderness and gives water in the wasteland. In other words, He will make a way where there seems to be no way!

Lord, sometimes it is hard for us to see what you are doing in our lives. Thank you for reminding us that you are doing something new. Help us not to fixate on the struggles and challenges of our yesterday that we miss the miracle of today.

STOP & THINK ABOUT IT

Blessed be the Lord, Who daily loadeth us with
benefits, Even the God of our salvation. Selah.
Psalm 68:19 (KJV)

H ave you ever stopped to think about how blessed you are? Seriously, have you? Did you wake up this morning? *That's a blessing.* If you are reading this, you have eyes to see and the ability to read. *That's a blessing.* It also means that you had the resources to purchase this book, or loved ones who blessed you with it. *Another blessing.* Sure, everything in your life may not be peachy keen, but who has a perfect life?

David pens this Psalm, praising God for being Israel's great deliverer. He invites the people to join him in praise. He opens the Psalm with a conquering cry, "Let God arise and His enemies be scattered!" Later, he extols God's attributes, calling Him a father to the fatherless and a defender of the widows. He points out that God gives homes to the homeless and liberates those in captivity. By the time we reach our focus verse, David has outlined how great and powerful God is. He exclaims, "Praise the Lord! Praise be to God our Savior!" David reminds us that God daily loads us up with benefits and we are fully supplied and carried by Him. He finishes the verse with the word *Selah*, which means to *pause* or *stop and think about it*.

Today, whether things in our lives are perfect or not, we need to stop and think about how blessed we are. We should take a moment to reflect on how far the Lord has brought us. Consider how many times we have been in danger and God protected us. Think about the times in which He extended His mercy and grace toward us instead of giving us the punishment we deserved. Every single day, God fully supplies us. He carries us, bears our burdens, lifts our heads, and supplies our needs. Stop and think about it...

Lord, thank you for loading us up with benefits every day. We offer our praises to you as we consider all that you have done for us. Today, we ask you for nothing and we thank you for everything.

JUST A WORD

He sent His word and healed them,
and delivered them from their destructions.
Psalms 107:20 (KJV)

People talk a lot. They talk about the problems in politics, failing educational systems, and ever increasing crime rates. No matter where you go, people are talking about something. Whether debating the latest game in the barbershop, dialoguing in the university lecture hall, or discussing in the produce section of the local grocery store, people are talking. Despite these debates, dialogues, and discussions, no one can seemingly come up with solutions. In our personal lives, people will give their opinions and suggestions about what we need to do or how we need to handle things. Some of this talking is helpful, and some (usually most of it) is unsolicited, unwarranted, and unneeded.

God doesn't have to do a lot of talking to get things done. There is so much power in what He says that He only needs a few words. The Bible is replete with examples of this truth. With a word, God creates the heavens and the earth. With a word, He creates mankind. With a word, He decimates the enemies of Israel. With a word, He stills turbulent storms, calms raging seas, and raises the dead. Liberation, exoneration, healing, and deliverance all come with just a word from God. And all it takes to change your life is a word from God.

Today, be determined to hear and heed what God says. He has the solution to every problem and the answer to every question we have. God holds the key to every door of opportunity we seek. The Psalmist reminds us today that God sends His word, and in that word comes healing and deliverance.

Dear God, we need to hear from you. Help us to drown out the sounds of things that are destructive to us. Open our ears to hear what you have to say.

AS YOU GO

And they lifted up their voices, and said,
Jesus, Master, have mercy on us.
And when he saw them, he said unto them,
Go shew yourselves unto the priests. And it came to pass,
that, as they went, they were cleansed.
Luke 17:13-14 (KJV)

Some things will never be manifested in our lives until we get up and go. Too often we allow our fears to paralyze us. We become gripped with the fear of failure or the fear of the unknown. Our minds become embroiled in a seemingly endless battle of questions. *How will this work? What if things don't go the way I thought they would? How can I do what God is showing me with all these issues I have?* Truthfully, the conditions in our lives will never be perfect. If we are waiting for everything to be perfect, we will never do what God is commanding us to do.

In our passage, Jesus is on His way to Jerusalem. He passes through an unnamed village and has an encounter with ten leprous men. They cry out for mercy, and Jesus tells them to show themselves to the priests. Culturally, these men are ostracized from their communities because of their illness. They must show themselves to the priest to return to their homes. While the Lord's response is culturally correct, it appears to be ill-timed. After all, nothing has happened yet. The miracle hasn't manifested; they are still lepers.

Have you, like those lepers, heard the Lord's command? Maybe God has told you to do something, and you can't figure out how to do it. Perhaps He is trying to do something in your life, and your fears are preventing you from receiving it. Beloved, hear the Word of the Lord. The key to your manifestation is found in your obedience. Just get up and go. Go believing that He will work it out. Go believing that if He called you to do it, He will supply what you need to accomplish it. Go knowing that God has the answers to all your questions.

Dear God, we acknowledge that we have heard your voice, but our fears have stopped us from obeying you. We cast down imaginations and take authority over every fear. Forgive us and help us to activate our faith once again.

GET UP FROM THERE

*And there were four leprous men
at the entering in of the gate:
and they said one to another,
Why sit we here until we die?
II Kings 7:3 (KJV)*

L ife doesn't always look or feel good. When facing challenges that seem insurmountable, it can be very easy to give up on life. Many people just decide that life is too difficult. They assess their current condition and conclude that they have simply had enough.

In our passage today, four lepers are sitting on the outside of the city gate. Inside, a horrible famine has gripped the city. Outside, the Syrian army has gathered preparing to attack. What a horrible dilemma. These men, pondering their predicament, ask themselves a very important question: Why sit here until we die? What a question. Considering their plight and the conditions around them, these men decide to get up and make a move. In the verses that follow, these men start walking toward the Syrian camp. As they go, God causes the Syrian army to hear what sounds like a great army marching toward them. Terrified at the prospect of inevitable defeat, the Syrians flee their camp, leaving food and treasure.

There is an alarm sounding that we need to hear. It's time to get up. We must not allow ourselves to "check out" of life. Yes, the problems are painful, and the outlook seems gloomy, but get up anyway. No, we don't have all the answers, but get up from there. Hear the Word of the Lord. You can begin again. It is not too late to get up and move on. As long as you have life, there is hope for a brighter future. Get up from there and keep living. Contrary to what the enemy would have you believe, you have not reached the end of your story. Get up and watch what God will do.

Lord, we thank you for your Word. Thank you for reminding us that we can get up from a painful place and live again. Help us to maintain our faith and trust in You.

LIVING WITH A LIMP

The sun rose upon him as he passed Penuel,
limping because of his hip.
Genesis 32:31 (ESV)

I t is amazing how powerful our perspective can be. Perspective is defined as a mental view or prospect. When we look at our lives, the lenses we choose to use to take that view can either lift or limit us. We all face difficulties, but how we see them is just as important as how we come out of them. In many cases, when we experience life-altering circumstances, we do not view them correctly and then find ourselves in a state of depression and disillusion.

In our passage today, Jacob has experienced a divine encounter that leaves him living with a limp. He has been left alone, preparing to meet Esau. Jacob must now come face to face with Esau, his brother, whose birthright he obtained through trickery and deception. The Bible records that Jacob wrestled with God all night long. He struggles while God changes his perspective and his name. Jacob continues to struggle until God knocks his hip out of joint.

Sometimes, like Jacob, God allows us to experience things that leave us scarred. When we find ourselves here, we must make sure that our perspective is correct. Beloved, hear the Word of the Lord. God is not punishing you; He is preparing you. God is not through blessing you. You may have a scar, but see it as a reminder that you are a survivor. After all, a scar is simply a mark left by a healed wound. Yes, you have been wounded, but you survived. It caused you to cry and made you want to give up, but you made it through. Now, see it for what it is, learn the lessons, and make your declaration, "I may be limping, but I'm still living!"

Father, thank you for allowing us to experience seasons of pain. We do not like it while we are going through it, but we know that we are in your hands and we trust you. Help us to keep the right perspective as you continue to prepare us to be all that you have declared that we will be. We love you and we thank you.

YOU CAN BEGIN AGAIN

This means that anyone who belongs
to Christ has become a new person. The old
life is gone; a new life has begun!
II Corinthians 5:17(NLT)

Occasionally, we all desire a new start. After certain experiences– both good and bad – it's normal to want to hit the reset button on life. In seeking out new beginnings, some people relocate; many move across town, out of state, or even out of the country. While others may change their name, friends, jobs, where they shop, and even the church they attend. Yes, we go through great measures to have a new beginning.

In our passage, the Apostle Paul is concerned with the believer's new life in Christ. Paul says that the love of Christ compels him to seek the salvation of everyone he meets. Furthermore, the love of Christ causes him not to judge a person based upon their external circumstances. He doesn't value a person based upon what they possess or what they have done. Why? The answer is simple. If any man is in Christ, he is a new person.

Perhaps you have made decisions in your life that aren't quite right. Be encouraged today. You CAN begin again. Don't listen to people who point to your past and attempt to use it against you. God does not see you the way they see you. If you have been wrestling with your past and are feeling like hope is lost, lift up your head. You can begin again!

Father, today we thank you for new beginnings. Because we are in you, we are new creations, with new lives. Thank you that the past is behind us and the slate is wiped clean. Help us to ignore the opinions of others and see ourselves as you see us.

PERSISTENT **PRAYER**

*Pray in the Spirit at all times and on
every occasion. Stay alert and be persistent
in your prayers for all believers everywhere.*
Ephesians 6:18 (NLT)

I sn't it amazing how we sometimes use prayer as a
last resort? If we are honest, we have all been guilty
of strategizing first and praying last. At the onset of
a problem, we make every attempt to solve our issues
with our knowledge, might, and readily accessible
resources. Typically, it is only after we have bumped our
heads or ran into a roadblock that we turn to prayer.

Paul writes to the Ephesian church that we need to
pray in the spirit at all times and on every occasion.
Simply put, there is never a reason we should not be
praying. This verse immediately follows Paul's
admonishment that we put on the whole the Armor of
God. He emphasizes that the armor is essential to
maintaining our defense against the enemy's attack.
Persistent prayer is just as essential.

To be persistent is to continue regardless of opposition, obstacles, or discouragement. The simple truth is that we must continue in prayer. Be persistent. Regardless of how challenging your circumstances may be, pray with persistence. Keep on praying. It may appear that nothing is happening, but don't stop praying. Your prayers energize your armor. The armor fits better with prayer. The shield is strengthened by prayer. Our use of the sword is sharpened through prayer. Beloved, chose today to develop a more persistent prayer life!

Father, we repent for using prayer as our last resort. Thank you for reminding us that we must persist or continue in prayer. Help us to develop and strengthen our prayer lives so that prayer is just as natural to us as breathing.

PRAYER CAN TURN IT

If my people, which are called by my name,
shall humble themselves, and pray, and
seek my face, and turn from their wicked ways;
then will I hear from heaven, and will
forgive their sin, and will heal their land.
II Chronicles 7:14 (KJV)

Our world is driven by the desire for advancement. We strive to achieve the best, obtain the latest, and discover the fastest. This unsettling desire for improvement can be seen in the constant growth of technology over the last 30 years. We have smaller mobile phones, smaller computers, and wireless internet service. You can stream your favorite television shows using wireless devices that fit into your pocket. You can even make telephone calls and see the person you're talking to. Although these are all great advances, sometimes the old method is the best method.

Our passage today gives us God's method for changing any situation. As Solomon is dedicating the Temple, the Lord speaks to him. God tells Solomon that He has accepted and chosen the temple to be His dwelling place. Further, God indicates that even when the children of Israel find themselves in the midst of judgment, there is a process by which all situations can be turned. If they humble themselves, pray, seek His face, and turn from their wicked ways, God promises to respond. He will hear from heaven, forgive their sins and heal their land.

We can agree that there is much sickness, sin, and disease in our land. However, we will not discover any new advancement to deal with it. Ask the politicians. For years, they have tried to fix things that only God can change. We are without the ability to make it happen any faster, nor can we find any devices to do the work for us. God calls His people back to prayer. Whatever situation you may be dealing with today, your turnaround will be found in prayer. Prayer can turn your finances around. It can heal your heart, lift your burdens, and remove your doubt. Prayer can change your mind. Prayer can turn the heart of your supervisor. Prayer can turn any situation around. Let's go back to prayer and allow God to take care of the rest.

Father, thank you for Your promise that if we would humble ourselves and pray, you would hear, forgive, and heal. We need your help today as we rededicate ourselves to you and your ways.

GOD IS ABLE

Now unto Him that is able to do exceeding
abundantly above all that we ask or think,
according to the power that works in us.
Ephesians 3:20 (KJV)

Have you ever looked at a situation and felt that it was too big? Have you ever prayed and questioned whether you would get an answer? Many times, we find ourselves in situations that are so overwhelming that praying seems like such a futile response. We wonder, *"Can God heal my broken heart? Can God repair my relationship with my children? Will my life ever get any better? Will I ever recover?"*

Paul writes to us, as he is concluding this prayer found in Ephesians 3, that God can do more than simply answer our prayers. He says that God can go above and beyond anything that we can ask or think. We serve an able God. We must believe this without any reservation. Secondly, we must have the courage to ask Him for what we want or need. Don't be afraid to lay it all on Him.

Sometimes, the problem is that we don't ask God for enough. We operate as if He is limited or weak. The Bible teaches us that we don't have what we want or need because we don't ask God for it.

God is powerful and limitless. His resources cannot be exhausted. Whatever your need may be, *ask Him.* Whatever your desires are, *tell Him.* Ask Him to heal your heart, repair your relationship, and show you the steps to take to change your life. *Just ask.* Stop treating God like He is fragile; you cannot break Him. He desires to help you. He stands ready to exceed your expectations. God wants to blow your mind with His blessings and favor. God is able!

Lord, thank you for reminding us today to simply ask you for what we want. We cast aside our fears and hesitations, knowing that no matter what we ask or think, you will exceed our expectations.

HE LEADS ME

He leadeth me in the paths of
righteousness for his name's sake.
Psalms 23:3b (KJV)

*S*avior lead me lest I stray – Gently lead me all the way – I am safe when by Thy side – I would in Thy love abide. Lead Me, Lead Me, Savior lead me lest I stray. Gently down the stream of time. Lead me Savior, all the way."

These lyrics, penned by Frank Davis in 1880, should echo the sentiments of every believers' heart as we traverse the varying terrain of our lives. Each of us experiences seasons when we are unsure of the Lord's direction. It is then that we must continue to trust in God's care and in His promise to lead us.

David writes in the 23rd Psalm that the *Lord leads us in the paths of righteousness for His name's sake.* Isn't it comforting to know that if we allow Him, God will be our navigator? The Lord leads us by His Word, through prayer, and even by closing doors. No matter how He leads, we can rely upon the truth that He will lead us. Even when He guides us into places that are uncomfortable, we can take comfort that He is ordering our steps.

Beloved, trust God to lead your life. Regardless of where you find yourself today, know that He will show you the way you should go. The Bible teaches us that we should trust and acknowledge God and when we do so, He will direct our paths.

Dear God, at times, we attempt to lead ourselves. In doing so, we often end up in places that we do not belong. We ask your forgiveness and we commit ourselves into your care. We trust that you will lead us and we thank you in advance for your guidance.

IT'S A QUESTION OF LOVE

After breakfast Jesus asked Simon Peter,
"Simon son of John, do you love me more than these?"
John 21:15a (NLT)

H*ow much do you love me?* What a question! People come up with all kinds of metaphoric responses to attempt an answer – especially when we have hurt or disappointed someone we love. If you have ever been asked that question, you know how dumbfounding it can be when your spouse or significant other looks you in the eyes and makes inquiry of the depth or measure of your love for them.

In the passage, Jesus is making a post-resurrection appearance on the banks of the Sea of Galilee. After feeding the disciples breakfast, Jesus has a conversation with Peter regarding the depth of his love. In their last conversation, Jesus tells of Peter's future denial. Now, having denied Christ and returned to fishing, Peter is face to face with Jesus and must respond to His question, *"Do you love Me more than these?"* Can you imagine Peter stuttering to answer? Jesus doesn't ask Peter about his *past failure*, He asks about his *present fidelity.*

Regardless of our current position or past failures, the Lord wants to know: *Do we really love Him?* Today, as we consider our relationship with God, remember that the real question is, if we love Him more than these? What exactly are *these?* Jesus is questioning if we love Him more than the people surrounding us, the positions we hold, popularity, fame, or fortune. Reflect upon these words from the hymn, *My Jesus I Love Thee,* "My Jesus, I Love Thee, I know that Thou art mine; For thee all the follies of sin I resign. My gracious Redeemer, my Saviour are Thou; if ever I loved Thee, my Jesus 'tis now."

Lord we love and praise you. Thank you for looking past our failures and mistakes. Help us as we seek to strengthen our love relationship with you.

PRAISE LOOKS GOOD ON YOU

Rejoice in the LORD, O ye righteous:
For praise is comely for the upright.
Psalm 33:1 (KJV)

A ll of us want to look our best. Some people maintain a strict diet and exercise daily to make sure they look good. Others will undergo medical procedures to remove wrinkles or enhance other physical features. We spend time shopping for just the right outfit to make us look as attractive as possible. We work to ensure that we stay abreast of the latest fashion trends to make sure that we are always "in style."

The Psalmist writes to us that praise is comely for the upright. The word *comely* is defined as pleasing in appearance, attractive, or fair. It is further defined as proper, seemly, or becoming. With that, no matter how you choose to define it, praise looks good on the believer. Praise is the natural response for us when we consider all the benefits the Lord gives to us.

Let's make praise part of our daily regimen. Our praises are attractive. What does praise attract? *Praise attracts God's presence.* The Bible says that God inhabits the praises of His people. Whenever we need the Lord to do something in our lives, we need to follow our prayers up with praise. When we praise, we speak to our circumstances and situations about our God. Our praises declare that our God is greater.

Lord, today we simply want to give you praise. We echo the sentiments of the psalmist, from the rising of the sun to the setting of the same, your name is worthy to be praised. We love you and we thank you.

FIRST THINGS FIRST

*Seek the Kingdom of God above all else,
and live righteously, and he will give you
everything you need.*
Matthew 6:33 (NLT)

Regardless of our particular stations in life, we all want to live the good life. While our specific definitions of a good life may be different, most of us would summarize by saying that we just want to be happy. We find ourselves going great lengths to achieve the happiness we desire. Some obsess over acquiring possessions, climbing the corporate ladder, or sculpting the perfect body. While others use alcohol and other recreational substances to ascend to a temporary state of euphoria. Somehow, in our attempt to capture it, happiness seems to elude us.

Jesus, in this portion of the Sermon on the Mount, is drawing a parallel between earthly possessions and heavenly possessions. Before our focus verse, He tells us to store our treasure in heaven because earthly treasures are subject to theft and decay. He talks about how God clothes the lilies and feeds the birds. Jesus then tells us that we should not be filled with worry or anxiety over any of our temporal needs. *If God takes care of the birds of the air and the flowers of the field, He will take care of us as well.* With that in mind, Jesus tells us that it is necessary that we prioritize or put first things *first.*

Is God and God's Kingdom a priority in your life? Beloved, there is nothing wrong with setting goals and achieving them. God is not against success by any means. He desires that we all be happy and successful, but not at the expense of ignoring Him and our responsibility in the Kingdom of God. The Word of God is clear. When we make God first, He will give us everything we need. And if you live right, He will not only supply your needs, but He will give you some of your wants too!

Lord, we desire to put first things first. Help us to identify those things that we have positioned incorrectly and make the necessary adjustments. Thank you for giving us the grace and strength we need to do what needs to be done.

STATION IDENTIFICATION

*This is what God the LORD says—
the Creator of the heavens, who
stretches them out, who spreads out
the earth with all that springs from it,
who gives breath to its people,
and life to those who walk on it:
Isaiah 42:5 (NIV)*

E very so often while listening to your favorite radio station, the announcer will pause to say or play a recorded announcement of the station identification. It may go a little something like, "This is Magic 1560 AM – WMRO, Gallatin, TN." While this is done primarily to remain in compliance with Federal Communications Commission (FCC) Regulations, station identification also lets us know what station or radio frequency we are tuned into so that we can find it again.

The Prophet Isaiah is living in severely idolatrous times. The children of Israel were often guilty of following other gods. Because they had been in

Babylonian captivity for an extended period, many felt that the cause of their captivity was due to the supremacy of the Babylonian idols. As a result, there were many Israelites who worshiped these idols. Additionally, many priests in Babylon claimed to represent or speak on behalf of one false god or another. God, knowing the minds of His people, chooses to identify Himself as Creator and Sustainer unequivocally. While there were many gods in Babylon, none of them could make that claim.

Today, just like then, we are surrounded by other voices, influences, things, and people that will attempt to rise to the level of God in our lives. Things like money, jobs, possessions, health, family, and even some friends can blur or distort our view of who God is. These things can become elevated because of the trust, reliance, dependence, and confidence we place in them. That's why station identification is imperative. There is only one God who can sustain us. When the other voices are silenced, He still speaks. When the other influences are powerless, He is still omnipotent. When the others are gone, He is still present. Check the station I.D!

Lord, thank you for reminding us of who you are. We commit to pulling down anything that we may have elevated too highly in our lives. Help us to identify these things and bring them subject to your will and your way.

PLANTED AND PROSPERING

*They are like trees planted along the
riverbank, bearing fruit each season.
Their leaves never wither, and they
prosper in all they do.*
Psalm 1:3 (NLT)

A farmer desiring maximum production from their crops will plant their seeds in the most fertile soil with the most irrigation. The farmer knows that these crops, regardless of any changing conditions, will be strong, stable, and fruitful.

In this Psalm, the lives of the righteous and the wicked are compared. The Psalmist begins by declaring how blessed or happy are those who choose to live Godly lives and refuse ungodly counsel, refrain from ungodly behavior, and take refuge from those who mock and scorn God. The Psalmist continues by pointing out that the believers' blessing or happiness comes from their delighting and meditating on the law – the principles, instructions, directions, or teachings – of the Lord. In doing so, the faithful are like trees planted by the river, bearing their fruit every season, never withering, and prospering in all that they do.

As believers, we have been planted. We have been set in place and established by the Lord to produce and prosper. As we continue to meditate on and delight ourselves in the Word of God, we will prosper in every way. The Lord promised Joshua that he would be prosperous and have success if he would continually meditate on and obey all of God's Word. Be encouraged to continue in the ways of God. Success and prosperity are already yours!

Lord, we appreciate the benefits of walking in your way. Help us as we continue to focus on your word. Thank you for planting us in good ground. We celebrate with great anticipation the blessings and successes that are already ours. We await expectantly on the manifestation of every promise.

FREE IN THE FIRE

He answered and said, Lo, I see four men
loose, walking in the midst of the fire,
and they have no hurt; and the form of the
fourth is like the Son of God.
Daniel 3:25 (KJV)

Have you ever felt trapped, chained, fettered, hindered, bound, or tied by circumstance? Fiery situations are challenges that are intensely provoking. Troubled marriages, broken relationships, and financial difficulties all have the propensity to become fiery frustrations. If left in these moments for too long, we begin to feel trapped inside an inescapable prison.

The story of Shadrach, Meshach, and Abednego, or the three Hebrew boys is familiar to many, especially those who have spent some time in or around the church. Nebuchadnezzar erected a golden image of himself and commanded that all the people worshiped it when the music played. These men refuse and find themselves being cast into a fiery furnace. Their complete confidence in God is tested at its ultimate level. They are thrown into the furnace bound, but God proves Himself faithful once again. God frees them while they are still in the fire.

Great deliverance does not always come in the form of escape. Sometimes, the greatest form of deliverance is being free while still in the fire. While we would rather that God remove the situation or move us, He will liberate us while we are still in it and give us the resources we need to withstand it. In our passage today, the Hebrew boys are still in the furnace, but they are free. Today, God sends His Word to remind us that we can indeed be free in the fire. Regardless of how difficult your challenges appear to be, allow the Lord to liberate your mind and your spirit. If God can free you while you're in it, there will be no problem getting you out of it!

Father, thank you for your Word today. We trust in your ability to set us free while we are still facing our own fiery furnaces. Help us to never forget that you are with us and will deliver us in it and out of it.

I DON'T EVEN LOOK LIKE IT

Then the high officers, officials, governors,
and advisers crowded around them and saw
that the fire had not touched them. Not a hair
on their heads was singed, and their clothing
was not scorched. They didn't even smell of smoke!
Daniel 3:27 (NLT)

Y*ou can't judge a book by its cover.* This familiar colloquialism is often used to remind us that judgments should not be made without taking a deeper or closer look at something. Another interpretation of this statement would be that you can't tell everything about a person just by observing their outward appearance.

Nebuchadnezzar, the king of Babylon, has erected a golden statue of himself. He commands that upon the playing of the instruments, all the people must bow and worship his image. The three Hebrew boys refuse to bow and are eventually cast into a fiery furnace. What should have resulted in their immediate death, became an opportunity for the Lord to show Himself strong on behalf of His servants. God not only frees them while in the furnace but delivers them without leaving any signs of them having ever been in it.

As we reflect upon this lesson, let's think about all of the challenges we have already survived. If it were up to the enemy, we would all be disillusioned, disenchanted and in a continual state of disappointment. In fact, for some, the mere fact that you aren't suicidal or stuck in some deep state of depression is a miracle. Life allows us to experience loss, heartache, heartbreak, sickness, and every other category of crisis. No one would ever know that we've been through so much in our lives. Despite everything we've been through, we keep a praise on our lips and in our hearts. We hold our heads up and keep a pep in our step. Why? The answer is simple. We've come THROUGH the fire. God brought us out, and we don't look like what we've been through!

Father, we thank you today for what you have done in our lives. Thank you that even when we are going through our trials, you have already determined when we will be delivered. Thank you that when we come out, we won't look like what we've been through.

LORD, DO YOU SEE THIS

*The eyes of the LORD watch over those who
do right; His ears are open to their cries for help.*
Psalm 34:15 (NLT)

How many times have you wondered if God was paying attention to what is happening around you? Poverty, pollution, wars, famine, genocide, corruption, manipulation, death, and destruction – *does God really see all this?* When struggling with difficulties and injustices in our own lives, we sometimes wonder if the Lord sees what is happening TO us as well.

Psalm 34 is believed to have been written by David after his escape from the Philistines in I Samuel 21. It opens with David's declaration to praise or *bless the Lord at all times.* David expresses his excitement over the truth that God heard his prayers and delivered him from trouble. Throughout this Psalm, David reminds us that while we will face many afflictions, trials, or

45

challenges as believers, God's eyes are watching, His hands are working, and His presence is prevailing.

Does God see what is happening in your life? Yes, He does. The Lord is keenly aware of every facet of your life and is concerned about you. Regardless of the circumstances you may be facing right now, you are not alone. The Lord's eyes are on you, and His ears are open to your cries. Instead of harboring your cares and concerns, cry out to Him for help. He sees your hurt and knows your pain. More importantly, He is infinitely powerful, His resources are unlimited, and He is able!

Father, thank you for reminding us that you are always watching us and working on our behalf. Sometimes, our outlook is gray as we face life's challenges. Help us to never forget your amazing love for us.

DON'T STOP PRAYING

And he spake a parable unto them to this end,
that men ought always to pray, and not to faint.
Luke 18:1 (KJV)

Prayer is the offering of petitions, supplications, and praises to God. As Christians, we are taught early about the importance of prayer. Many of us were told to say our prayers before we went to bed. We were taught the Model or Lord's Prayer in our Sunday School classes. We have listened to deacons and preachers pray during worship experiences. Some of us were even fortunate enough to hear our parents and grandparents pray at home. Unfortunately, as we heard prayer, no one told us that praying is not always easy. No one mentioned that sometimes, you don't feel like praying. It is easy to offer prayers in church, but it is another thing to have a consistent prayer life at home.

Luke 18 opens with Jesus teaching on persistence in prayer. In the verses that follow, He gives a parable about a widow and an unjust judge. Although the judge continually disregards her petition, she never ceases to come seeking justice. Have you ever felt disregarded by God? At times, when we are praying about something and heaven is silent, it's hard to keep praying. It is during those seasons that we must be persistent in our prayers. In the passage, the judge eventually relents and avenges her because of her persistence.

Jesus teaches us that we should always pray and not faint or lose heart. The enemy of our souls would prefer that we accept defeat and believe that God doesn't hear or care about our concerns. The devil is a liar. God cares. He will answer in His own time. Remember what the saints of old taught us: *He may not come when we want Him, but He is always on time.* Though our trials are great and the way gets hard, God wants us to be persistent in prayer.

Father, we admit that at times, it is hard to keep praying. Help us to develop consistent prayer lives. We thank you in advance for hearing and answering us.

IRREVERSIBLE

Yes, and from ancient days I am he.
No one can deliver out of my hand.
When I act, who can reverse it?"
Isaiah 43:13 (NIV)

A doctor walks into a patient's hospital room and says, "It appears that you've made a full recovery. We thought the cancer had returned, however, the cells have completed disappeared. It is unlikely that they will return." Certain that the doctor's prognosis is final and absolute, the patient accepts the report and shifts their thoughts to managing life anew without the fear of cancer ever returning.

Isaiah is prophesying of the great deliverance that God will give to the Nation of Israel following the Babylonian captivity. From the fortieth chapter, Isaiah powerfully describes God as redeemer, restorer, protector, and guide. Particularly, within our specific focus verse, God reminds them that He is God. He always was God and that He always will be God. This verse can be summarized by simply saying that God is sovereign.

God has supreme rank, power, and authority. As such, He says that there isn't anything that can be taken from Him, and there is no one who can reverse His actions.

The Lord is at work in our lives. He always has been. Saving, protecting, guarding, and guiding; He has always been working on our behalf. Even more, God has been blessing us, and His blessings are irreversible. No matter who or what has been attempting to sabotage what God is doing in our lives, we can take courage! God's blessings are irreversible. Just like that patient, we must fully accept the report of the Lord and shift our focus to live to know that what God has done, is doing, and what He will do is irreversible.

Father, we accept and believe your report. Thank you for your irreversible blessings. We acknowledge that you have been working in our lives all along. Help us to remain courageous in the face of every challenge, knowing that you are sovereign.

PURSUE & RECOVER

And David inquired at the LORD, saying,
Shall I pursue after this troop? Shall I overtake them?
And he answered him, Pursue: for thou shalt
surely overtake them, and without fail recover all.
I Samuel 30:8 (KJV)

Have you ever had something stolen from you? You leave home with everything intact, only to return to find that someone has invaded your space and taken your belongings. You call the police and quickly assess the situation to discover what has been taken. What an emotional roller-coaster ride. You start this ride feeling fear and panic and end it with anger and resentment.

David and his mighty men return to their homes to find that it has been destroyed by the Amalekites. Their wives and children have been taken captive, and all their possessions have been burned. Amidst their grief, David seeks God for direction. God tells David to pursue and recover. In verses 18-19, you will find that David did indeed recover everything that was stolen and nothing was missing.

Each of us will face losses in our lives. Our passage today teaches us that we must seek God's direction when dealing with moments like these. In fact, the book of Proverbs teaches us that we should acknowledge God in all our ways and that He will direct our paths. Hear the Word of the Lord. Pray and obey. The devil is a thief, and he comes to steal everything God gives to us. However, our story doesn't have to end there. If God says to pursue, we must go after it with all our might. Just like He did for David, God will give us the resources we need to recover everything the devil has stolen.

Lord, thank you for empowering us. Thank you for reminding us that we can recover all. Stir our faith and determination as we pursue and recover the things that we have lost.

WHAT'S IN YOUR HAND

Then the LORD asked him, "What is that in your hand?"
"A shepherd's staff," Moses replied.
Exodus 4:2 (NLT)

Following God is not always easy, especially when God is calling you to do what seems to be impossible. Answering His call often produces great joy and great fear. We feel great joy in realizing that God calls us despite our many shortcomings. There is joy in knowing that He has no respect of persons and will use anyone who presents themselves to Him as living sacrifices. Answering the call of God can also produce fear. Upon hearing the call of God we wonder, *"What if I mess up? What if I don't have any supporters? How will I accomplish what He is asking of me"?*

In our passage, Moses is responding to God's call to lead the children of Israel out of Egypt. Moses has seen the burning bush and heard God's voice. Now, here he stands in the presence of God dealing with the fears that come along with saying yes to God. *What if the people don't believe? What if they say that you never appeared to me?* God responds to Moses by asking, "What is that in your hand?"

The greatest evidence of our encounter with God is not eloquent speech. It is not in our pious demeanor or church rhetoric and jargon. No, the greatest evidence is in what God does through us, using the gifts and talents He has given to us. Let us be mindful not to waste time looking for external validation and support. God wants us to use what He has placed in our hands. The Lord has given each of us skills, abilities, gifts, and talents. It is His desire and our responsibility to take them, cultivate, and grow them for use in the Kingdom of God. What's in YOUR hand?

Lord, you have given us abilities that we have not used to benefit your Kingdom. We ask for your forgiveness. Help us to cultivate and grow our gifts and talents so that you will be glorified.

APPRECIATING **AFFLICTION**

It is good for me that I have been afflicted;
That I might learn thy statutes.
Psalm 119:71(KJV)

Hindsight is 20/20. Have you ever heard that before? It is a statement typically made when an individual looks back on a particular situation and sees clearly what they could not see while going through it. It is very difficult to see benefits or blessings while enduring painful experiences. At some juncture, each of us will experience seasons of disappointment, heartbreak, sickness, and loss. During these moments, it is easy to grow weary, angry, resentful, and bitter.

David, our writer, has every right to make this declaration in scripture. Surely, he can relate to having to deal with many afflictions. When the Prophet Samuel comes to his father's house looking for the next king of Israel, David's father counts him out. After David was celebrated for defeating Goliath, King Saul repeatedly tried to kill him. As a result of Saul's displeasure, David is forced to leave his home and live with the Philistines. During his life, David faced betrayals, attacks, and judgment. In this passage, he wrote that it was all good.

Perhaps, as you read this, you are facing some of the most challenging experiences of your life. The pain is great, and the problems are many. Hear the Word of the Lord. Your pain is not punishment; it is preparation. Some lessons cannot be learned through moments of ease and comfort. We learn that God is a healer through sickness. We learn that He is a provider through seasons of lack. When we experience loneliness, we learn that God will never leave us. When we are at our wit's end, we learn that He is a peace giver. We can appreciate the seasons of affliction in our lives because they teach us about our great God.

Father, it is difficult to appreciate the painful places in our lives. Help us to see that you are using each of these experiences to perfect us. It is our desire to learn all that you are trying to teach us. We thank you, even in these seasons because we know that they will not last forever.

CHOICES

Trust in the LORD with all your heart;
do not depend on your own understanding.
Seek His will in all you do, and He will show
you which path to take.
Proverbs 3:5-6 (NLT)

L ife is filled with a multiplicity of opportunities to make choices. Each morning we awaken to a new day with new choices to make. *What will I wear today? What will I eat for breakfast? Which route will I take to work? What will I tackle first?* As the day progresses, we find ourselves making choices about everything. Some choices are rather simplistic. *What should I eat for lunch? Should I buy this new outfit?* While others require a bit more thought. *Should I respond to that text? Should I answer that call? Should I REALLY say what I want to say?*

Occasionally, we find ourselves wishing that all the necessary choices are made for us before we wake up in the morning. Breakfast is prepared, clothes are ironed, no issues on the job, spouse or significant other is good, and the children are behaving. The frustrations of having to consider what to do, when to do it, and how to do it can mount up until we throw up our hands in desperation and say, "I DON'T CARE!"

Beloved, remember that we are not journeying through our lives all alone. God has promised that as we continue to trust and seek Him, He will show us exactly what we need to do. When you don't know what to say, ask Him. When you aren't sure about which path to take, seek His direction. And when He doesn't answer when or how you'd like Him to, trust Him.

Father, we acknowledge your presence and ask for your help as we make our choices today. We ask you to direct us and we trust you with the outcomes.

IT'S A SET UP

And we know that all things work together
for good to them that love God, to them
who are the called according to his purpose.
Romans 8:28 (KJV)

God is setting you up for something great. That sounds really good, doesn't it? The problem is, it often may not feel like it. Sometimes we find ourselves reeling and rocking from the many twists and turns that life brings. Lost jobs, broken relationships, and financial pressures all have a way of making us question this proposition that God is setting us up for something great. It even feels like we cannot sense God's Presence while we are going through these trials.

Truthfully, not everything that happens to us in life is good, but all things work together FOR our good. This is important to remember. No, having our lives turned upside down by some sudden, unexpected change, illness, or some other catastrophic event may not be good per se. As believers, we are not given immunity from the challenges of life, but we do have a promise. God will bring good out of every bad situation we face.

Perhaps, as you read this, you are growing weary. You have been hit with a series of challenges that seem to come one right after the other. God's Word for you today is that it is all working in your favor. God is using every circumstance, good and bad, to prepare you for His purposes. Despite what you're going through, God's promises are faithful and true. You are being set up for greatness. No, I cannot tell you HOW it will work out, but I KNOW that it will.

Father, thank you for your promise. Help us to maintain our faith while you are working on our situation. We reaffirm our trust in you and your Word. Thank you in advance that it is all working together for our good.

SPEAK TO IT

And He said unto me, Son of man,
can these bones live? And I answered,
O Lord GOD, thou knowest. Again He said
unto me, Prophesy upon these bones, and say
unto them, O ye dry bones, hear the Word of the Lord.
Ezekiel 37:3-4 (KJV)

As children, we are encouraged to take advantage of every opportunity to ensure that we are successful. We are taught to use good posture, display proper etiquette, and pay attention in our classes. We graduate from high school, and some of us continue to college. We do all of this in hopes of having a good life. Sometimes, however, even with all our preparation, we find ourselves in less than desirable situations.

Our protagonist in the passage finds himself placed in a valley full of dry bones. Here's the kicker: God brought him to that valley. Usually, when we think about God and God's plans for us, we think about wealthy or prosperous places. We think about places where we can make a significant impact and be appreciated for our efforts. Rarely, if ever, do we expect to be brought to a place like this valley of dry bones. God brings Ezekiel to this valley and then commands him to speak to them.

Occasionally, we too find ourselves in the same valley. No, we don't see dry bones, but we do see situations that appear dead and lifeless. Some of us see this in our homes, on our jobs, in our communities, and sadly, even in our churches. Typically, our initial response is that either we have done something wrong or God has made a mistake. As such, we would much rather run in retreat than to stay and speak to that which seems impossible. However, let us hear and heed the Word of the Lord. It is time to speak. Speak life to that situation. Don't just speak empty words, but make a faith-filled declaration. By the time Ezekiel had finished speaking, a mighty army had stood before him. Just as God used Ezekiel, God desires to do the same with us. Nothing will happen until you speak.

Lord, we accept our assignment today and we align ourselves with your Word. Regardless of how things look around us, we will not retreat. Help us to strengthen our faith as we boldly speak life into our relationships, homes, communities, and churches.

FINDING YOUR WAY

Jesus saith unto him, I am the way,
the truth, and the life: no man cometh
unto the Father, but by me.
John 14:6 (KJV)

B eing lost is a terrible experience, particularly when you thought you knew where you were going. You ignore the people who try to tell you which way to go because you already know where you are headed – or so you thought. Worse yet, being lost becomes especially difficult when you have the wrong directions. The discovery that your GPS or printed directions are incorrect leaves you feeling helpless and vulnerable.

In today's passage, Jesus is comforting his disciples as they struggle with the news that he was going to be leaving them soon. The very idea was agonizing. These disciples have walked with Jesus for nearly three years. They have witnessed miracle after miracle. From the dead being raised to feeding the multitude with a little boy's lunch. He has taught them everything they know, and now they are faced with the reality that their teacher was not going to be with them much longer. At one point in the passage, Jesus tells them that they know the way He is going. Thomas speaks up to tell Jesus that they don't know where He is going and they really don't know the way.

The path of life has some confusing twists. All of us strive to find our way through the many situations we cross paths with. We must find our way through all of life's many challenges. Through hard trials, tribulations, and persecutions, *we search.* Through sickness and pain, *we seek.* We look for the way in self-help books. We speak with our friends in hopes that they will point us in the right direction. Jesus tells us very clearly that He is the way. Trust Him. If you are dealing with a dark situation that you can't see your way through, trust God; He is your way out, over, and through.

Father, thank you for being the way, the truth, and the life. As we traverse the challenging roads in our lives, help us to always remember that you are the way.

YOUR VICTORY IS IN THE BAG

*Then he took his staff in his hand,
chose five smooth stones from the stream,
put them in the pouch of his shepherd's bag and,
with his sling in his hand, approached the Philistine.*

1 Samuel 17:40 (NIV)

What a great feeling it is to know that your victory is secured! You don't have the resources that others have. You're not as strong or experienced. You're the underdog, and no one expects you to win. In fact, many think you're crazy for even trying. Somehow, you continue to thrive and excel in the face of incalculable odds.

David is preparing to face Goliath in battle. What a ridiculous match-up. Can you imagine an inexperienced civilian going out in head-to-head combat with an experienced soldier? Scholars suggest that David was anywhere from 17-20 years old when he faced Goliath. Here is this young shepherd with nothing but five stones and a slingshot. It's a suicide mission for sure. Goliath is a seasoned soldier who has been fighting since his adolescence. He's armed with a sword and shield. There is no way he can lose. Despite being scolded by his brother and initially rejected by Saul, David is confident that God will give him victory over Goliath. With one stone from his bag, he takes down Goliath and then uses Goliath's sword to finish the job.

Like David, your victory is already guaranteed! You may be the underdog in the situation, but the victory still belongs to you. Stop looking at what you don't have and use what's in your bag. You may not have enough finances, friends, or followers, but if you have faith – you've got what you need! Be encouraged; your victory is in the bag.

Father, thank you for securing our victory in every area of our lives! We do not run from our challenges; we face them in faith. Thank you for reminding us that you have supplied us with the tools we need to defeat every giant we encounter.

THIRSTING FOR GOD

As the deer pants for the water brooks,
So pants my soul for You, O God.
Psalm 42:1 (NKJV)

Thirst is defines as a strong desire, yearning, craving or longing for something or someone. Have you ever been thirsty? A cold glass of lemonade on a hot summer day or the taste of some sweet treat while trying to stick to a diet would quench your thirst. You want it so badly that you can almost taste it. Even more, the desire to be in the presence of someone you love can be overwhelming. That longing can become so intense that the memory of their voice pierces the silence that surrounds you. Thirst is a powerful force.

The Psalmist is grief-stricken because he was unable to go to Jerusalem. Many scholars believe this Psalm was written somewhere near Mount Hermon, which would place the Psalmist at a great distance away from his desired location. The pilgrimage to Jerusalem during the feasts was signally important. The people would overlook the possibility of robbery, heat exhaustion, and even death just to get to the temple. Our writer, unable to make the journey, feels separated from the temple and alienated from the presence of God.

The deer pants for the water brook to quench its thirst and to hide its scent from the predator. The deer knows that there is life and safety in the water. As believers, our lives are held together by the time we spend in the presence of God. There is help and healing found in His presence. Today, commit yourself to seeking and searching for God.

Father, our souls long for your presence. We commit our ways and direct our thoughts to you. Help us as we continue to seek and search for Your Will to be accomplished in our lives. We want to be all that you have destined for us to be.

LORD, I BELIEVE

Jesus said unto him, If thou canst believe,
all things are possible to him that believeth.
Mark 9:23 *(KJV)*

We live in a society that seems to be dominated by people who simply do not believe in much of anything. Can we really blame them? To believe is to have confidence or faith in the truth, existence, or the reliability of something. Broken promises by parents, politicians, and even preachers have left many wondering who can be trusted. Lost jobs, foreclosures, scandals, and scams all lead us down a path of disbelief. Is there anyone or anything left that we can count on?

The father in this passage has a son with a serious problem. He takes his child to the disciples, but they are powerless to help. Can you imagine the scene as Jesus comes walking up? This man, believing that he has come to the right place, is now distraught wondering who will help his child. At that moment, Jesus shows up. This father, cautiously, asks Jesus to help his son if he can. He responds, "If you can believe, all things are possible."

Perhaps as you read this, you are dealing with your own predicament. You, like this father, have talked to the people you thought could help. Now, you find yourself wondering whether there is anyone left for you to count on. Maybe your issue is so large that you are too overwhelmed to even speak to anyone about it. Regardless of what you may be facing, the key to your deliverance is to believe.

As people of faith, we must believe and keep on believing. You must believe that God has a plan for your life. Believe that God will turn that situation around. Believe that God is still in control. Believe that you will have victory. Believe that it's going to work together for your good. Believe and keep on believing. All things are possible to him that believes.

Lord, sometimes our faith is challenged and we get a little shaky. Help us in our moments of unbelief. Thank you for always showing up just in time. Our declaration henceforth and forever shall be, "I believe!"

GRACE **TO FORGET**

*Brethren, I count not myself to have apprehended:
but this one thing I do, forgetting those things
which are behind, and reaching forth unto those
things which are before,*
Philippians 3:13 (KJV)

Memorization is taught to us early in life. As children, we work to remember the names of our extended family members. We go on to school and learn the alphabet, spelling, and arithmetic. We are told to memorize the multiplication tables. We are taught skills to help us remember. Tools like mnemonic devices and word associations are used to help trigger our memories. We work very hard to remember. Strangely enough, as difficult as it seems to remember some of these things, we often struggle to forget too.

In the verses before our focus scripture, Paul is writing to the Philippian church about his background. He talks about his lineage as a Benjamite, his training as a Pharisee, and his zealousness to defend his faith. He concludes that, although he could boast in his ancestral heritage, it pales in comparison to the inheritance he has received in Christ. Further, he adds that while he is striving to deepen his relationship with God, he has not yet reached perfection. Which brings us to our targeted verse. Paul says *I have not yet obtained or apprehended this perfection, but this is what I do, I forget what is behind me.*

Let us accept, adopt, and appreciate the grace to forget. Perhaps we need to release our past successes so that we do not sabotage our future by resting on our laurels. Maybe we need to forget previously painful places so that we can embrace God's promises for a brighter future. Regardless of what our past may be, today we must make a conscious decision to stop living in it. There is nothing we can do about the past but learn from it. We cannot repair it, and we cannot relive it. Embrace the grace to forget. Look forward, with great expectation, to what God is doing with your today and tomorrow.

Lord, help us today to release ourselves from our past. Thank you for the grace to forget and move forward with our lives. We thank you for what you are doing in our lives today and look forward with great expectation to what you will do with our tomorrows.

IT WON'T WORK

*No weapon that is formed against thee
shall prosper; And every tongue that shall
rise against thee in judgment thou shalt
condemn. This is the heritage of the servants
of the LORD, And their righteousness
is of me, saith the LORD.*

Isaiah 54:17 (KJV)

The enemy is always looking for weapons to use against us. Sometimes he uses things we are familiar with. Financial hardships, broken friendships, and failing relationships are common occurrences we all face from time to time. However, there are other times in which the enemy will use weapons we don't expect or anticipate. Unexpected illnesses and sudden job losses tend to knock us to our knees. We may even experience disappointment and discouragement from family members, friends, and co-workers who speak negatively about us, our circumstances, dreams, goals, and aspirations. These weapons are "formed" to keep us in a negative cycle or mental state.

In the passage, the prophet Isaiah reminds us that although weapons will be formed against us, they will not prosper. The nation of Israel receives assurance from God that following the period of judgment they are currently experiencing, restoration will come. What a great word to receive! You and I can also rejoice that despite our mistakes and failures, God won't allow the "weapons" being used against us to prosper. If we continue to seek the face of God, like Israel, He will restore us again. Isn't that good news?

Beloved, be encouraged! Know that God will not allow the enemy's attacks against you to prosper. Know that even when you face a weapon, test, or trial you have never experienced before, God will give you the victory. His promise stands sure. *No weapon!* Forsaken by true enemies? *No weapon!* Struggling with your past? *No weapon!* Crying yourself to sleep? *No weapon!* Hold on, trust God, and anticipate a victorious ending.

Father, thank you for reminding us that no weapon formed against us will prosper. Help us to maintain our faith while we wait on your promise be manifested.

BE STEADFAST

*Therefore my beloved brethren, be ye steadfast,
unmovable always abounding in the work
of the Lord, forasmuch as ye know that your
labour is not in vain in the Lord.*
I Corinthians 15:58 (KJV)

There are some things that we just know. When we know *that we know*, we cannot be persuaded from our position. No one could convince us that we don't know our names or how old we are. We just know. When someone tries to give us directions to travel someplace we've been before, we stop them because we already know how to get there. Even in settings where someone we know is being introduced, we will skip the formalities because we already know them.

There is a confidence that comes with knowing. When we know a person's character, it is difficult for our opinion of them to be swayed by rumors. Regardless of anything that may be said, we remain resolute about them because we know them. In fact, we will jump to their defense because we know them. What do we know about God?

In today's passage, we are encouraged to be both steadfast and unmovable. Steadfast refers to being firm or resolute in faith, while unmovable can be defined as something that cannot be influenced regardless of feelings, circumstances, or emotions. There will be moments when doubt, disappointment, and disbelief will attempt to move us. The enemy will try to overthrow our faith by telling us things that are in opposition to the promises of God. He will tell us that we cannot win, we will not be healed, and what we believe for will never come to fruition. Be encouraged and be steadfast in those moments. Be confident in what you know about God and His character. Be steadfast and declare to the enemy, "I shall not be moved!"

Most Gracious God, we thank you for knowing who you are. For knowing that you have a plan and purpose for our lives. We commit ourselves to be firm in our faith and immovable in our position.

WHAT'S IN YOUR MOUTH

*I will bless the LORD at all times; His praise
shall continually be in my mouth.*
Psalm 34:1 (KJV)

This verse could easily be one of the most quoted verses in the Bible. It is quoted in songs. Many worship leaders and ministers use this verse as part of their call to worship. Even I, in a moment of intensified worship, will shout out from the pulpit with much vim and vigor this familiar passage to an ecstatic group of worshippers. Typically, the response is one of much excitement that leads to shouts of "Hallelujah," "Glory to God," and other exultant praises.

What about when we aren't in church? Life presents us with plenty of opportunities to gripe, grumble, and complain. It's easy to keep praises in our mouths when we are gathered together in church or surrounded by other like-minded believers. However, when we're at work, and the boss is working our last nerve, what's in our mouths then? When the children have gone crazy, money is funny, change is strange, coffee is cold, and toast is burned, what do we declare during those moments? Is it possible to bless the Lord at ALL times?

The challenge set before us is to develop and maintain a constant habit of praise. I know, it sounds impossible. Much like any other lifestyle or habit change, we will have to be determined to make it happen. When presented with opportunities to gripe about how terrible things are in your life, raise a praise instead. Even if it's an "anyhow" or "in spite of" praise, *raise it.* Your praises will do more for you than your complaining ever will. Raise a praise and watch your praise raise you!

Lord, help us to keep a praise in our mouths. Don't allow us to replace our praises with complaints as we face the challenges of each new day.

WE HAVE THIS TREASURE

But we have this treasure in earthen vessels,
that the excellency of the power may be of God,
and not of us.
II Corinthians 4:7 (KJV)

Where do you put your treasure? We place great emphasis upon protecting our valuable possessions. We put them in safety deposit boxes in the bank or fire proof lock boxes neatly tucked away in our homes. We buy insurance policies to protect them in case of theft or damage. We want to ensure that if anything happens to us, our treasures are preserved for our descendants. Makes a lot of sense, right?

The Apostle Paul, writing to the Corinthian church, wrote that God had given us the light of the Gospel. In fact, Paul says that God, who spoke light out of darkness in creation, chooses to deposit this light into jars of clay. Consider the confidence that God places in us. He communicates and entrusts the light of His Word to fragile vessels, prone to disobedience. He trusts vessels He knew would miss the mark time after time. Despite our many shortcomings, He gives us His treasure. Why does God do this? *So that the world can see that our great power comes from Him and is not conjured up by ourselves.*

Beloved, God uses each of us to receive and reflect the light of the Gospel. We have this treasure. What we have obtained from God far exceeds the value of anything else we can ever possess. This treasure soothes doubts and calms fears. This treasure lifts burdens and gives peace in times of storm. We have this treasure that even shines through the cracks in our lives. This treasure that takes our individual flaws and transforms us into vessels of honor.

Father, thank you for entrusting us with the light of the Gospel of Jesus Christ. Help us to never do anything that will discredit you and your Kingdom. We desire to be vessels that you can use to reflect Your Glory in the Earth.

I AM CONFIDENT

And this is the confidence that we have in Him, that, if we ask any thing according to His will, He heareth us:

I John 5:4 (KJV)

Confidence is defined as the full trust or belief in the powers, trustworthiness, or reliability of a person or thing. As we look around us, there are not a lot of things we can place our confidence in. We continue to be consistently overwhelmed by news of police brutality, political scandal, legal injustices, and increasing racial tensions. Furthermore, many of our lives are troubled. We struggle with broken relationships and broken promises; our hearts fragile and filled with fear.

In the face of all this negativity and uncertainty, as believers, we maintain our confidence in God. We have this confidence because our God is immutable. He is changeless. Our confidence is secure because God is consistent. Our confidence in God cannot be shaken because we know He cares for us. Our passage points out that our confidence rests in the knowledge that when our prayers and petitions agree with the Word of God, He hears us.

What do you need God to do in your life? What areas of uncertainty are you facing? Remember that our God is faithful. Sometimes, we must face difficult situations that we simply do not understand. We attempt to find someone to explain, but their attempts are meager at best. However, while we do not always understand the ways of God, we can be confident in His ability to lead and direct our lives. Be confident that you are in the plan of God. Know that God knows what He is doing. When you find yourself needing some answers or direction, be confident that if you ask Him according to His will, He hears you.

Great God, we praise your name today. You are an awesome God and we simply want to thank you for being so trustworthy. We affirm our faith in you and your ability to lead and direct our lives. Thank you, Lord, for what you have done, what you are doing, and what you will do in each of us.

RESTORATION

And I will restore to you the years that
the locust hath eaten, The cankerworm,
and the caterpillar, and the palmerworm, My
great army which I sent among you.
Joel 2:25 (KJV)

I sn't it amazing how time flies? Particularly when we
look at our lives and take inventory of how much
time we've lost. When we are young, we make large
plans to do incredible things. We plan to finish school,
have a great career, and travel the world. Then, we blink
and years have flown by. Our lives have taken us on a
journey we hadn't planned for. Now we are dealing with
stuff that sometimes makes us look back and scratch our
heads trying to figure out what happened and where all
the time went.

In our passage, Joel is conveying a message from God
regarding the restoration of Israel. They have been
devastated by a locust plague that was followed up by a

drought and famine. These horrible circumstances were brought about as a result of their continued disobedience. In the midst of these horrific conditions, God sends a word of hope and a message of restoration to them.

Today, perhaps you find yourself facing conditions that are less than perfect. Know that God is a God of restoration. While it is true that WE cannot create more than 24 hours in a day, God has a way of helping us to make up for lost time. Regardless of whether your circumstances are the result of disobedience, procrastination, or happenstance, don't allow the enemy to trick you into believing that it's too late! God desires to restore to you the time you've lost. Turn to Him believing in His promises, listening to His directions, and watching with great anticipation. God does what seems impossible.

Lord, thank you for restoration. We repent of every act of disobedience, hesitation, and procrastination. We align ourselves with your Word and thank you in advance for helping us make up the time. We await your directions knowing that with you, nothing is impossible.

THE DOOR IS OPEN

*I know all the things you do, and I have
opened a door for you that no one can
close. You have little strength, yet you
obeyed my word and did not deny me.*

Revelation 3:8 (NLT)

God is at work on your behalf. He is fully aware of all that you do and will never forget your sacrifice and labor of love. That is especially important to remember when you're dealing with people. Sometimes, people forget. They forget how you have been there for them. Regardless of how thankful they may have been initially, as time passes, people tend to forget. They forget how much you've sacrificed your time, talent, and treasure.

Our focal point today is derived from the letter to the Church at Philadelphia. The church at Philadelphia was a good church. If its name implies its character, it was a loving church. It was also a church that faced much opposition. In the face of opposition, it remained faithful, obedient, and persevering. The Lord sends a message of encouragement to this church, reminding them that He knows their works and is aware of everything going on around them. He rewards their obedience and faithfulness by opening a door that no one can close.

Beloved, God is completely aware of you and your circumstances. Regardless of the challenges occurring in your life right now, remain faithful and obedient to Him. His promise applies to you. You may be forgotten by those you have labored to help along the way, but be faithful. God will reward you by opening doors and creating opportunities that no one can hinder. In fact, look around you...the door IS open.

Thank you Lord for reminding us that you are aware of all that is going on in our lives. We commit to remain faithful and obedient servants to you. We wait with earnest expectation, looking for the doors that you will open, and the opportunities that you will create.

ACKNOWLEDGEMENTS

I want to acknowledge the hard work and dedicated assistance of everyone who worked to make this book a reality. Special thanks to:

The staff of Umiko D. Jones Sr. Ministries
Jessica, Akela, and the entire Keen Vision Publishing team
Tramayne Wright and the Studio 5 Agency

BISHOP UMIKO D. JONES SR.

UDJONES
MINISTRIES

Umiko D. Jones Sr., is the Senior Pastor of Gravel Hill Missionary Baptist Church in Bethpage, Tennessee. An accomplished author, Christian educator and expositor of the gospel; his wealth of knowledge and experience has garnered the respect of leaders in both secular and Christian arenas. He is a gifted preacher and teacher of the Word of God and has been privileged to minister across denominational lines, leading revivals, workshops and seminars around the country.

He is a proud member of Phi Beta Sigma Fraternity, Incorporated and a Subscribing Life Member of the National Association for the Advancement of Colored People (NAACP).

A native of Milwaukee, WI, Umiko currently resides in Murfreesboro, TN with his children. To learn more about Umiko, his family, and his ministry, visit www.umikojones.org.

STAY CONNECTED

Thank you for purchasing Words Along the Way. Umiko would like to connect with you! Below are a few ways you can connect with him. Follow, email, and visit today to stay posted on new releases, book signings, speaking engagements, and more!

FACEBOOK BishopUDJonesSr
INSTAGRAM UDJonesSr
YouTube UDJonesSr
WEBSITE www.umikojones.org
EMAIL info@umikojones.org